Let Advent be Advent

VINCENT SHERLOCK

First published in 2017 by Messenger Publications

The right of Vincent Sherlock to be identified as the author of the Work has been asserted by him in accordance with the Copyright and Related Rights Act, 2000.

ISBN 9781910248805

Designed by Messenger Publications Design Department
Typeset in Baskerville
Printed by Nicholson & Bass Ltd

Messenger Publications,
37 Lower Leeson Street, Dublin 2
www.messenger.ie

Through a chink too wide
there comes in
no wonder.

— From 'Advent' by Patrick Kavanagh

Contents

Let Advent be Advent

There are some who
want us to think that it's Christmas Eve,
with just five minutes left before shops close.
Has all this replaced Advent?
The answer is no.
The Advent wreath is before us,
the journey is beginning afresh
and we'll take it all with us to
the door and straw of the Bethlehem stable and,
on Christmas Day,
we'll celebrate as if for the first time
the Birth of
our Saviour.

Introduction

What Matters are you Discussing as you Walk Along?

Thank you for picking up this book. I hope that between now and the end of the Advent season you might have picked it up, put it down, forgotten where you've left it and found it many times!

In the pages that follow, I have offered some thoughts to accompany the days leading us to the celebration of Christmas. Advent calls us to prepare a room for the Lord so that he may truly be welcomed into our hearts and allowed to grow from the newborn child into the one who walked the way marked out for him and, on that walk, called (and still calls) others to join him.

This booklet, in many ways, lacks structure. By which I mean, some of the days coincide with the liturgy of the day and borrow from the Scripture passages used on those days at Mass. Other days are not linked with Scripture and, even where they are, the passage may well not correspond with the Church's chosen passages. Some of the thoughts are random reflections that might help you to ponder the script of your own life and your place on the Christian journey. Others are developed from a scriptural starting point. The days are laid out according to the weeks of Advent and the final days of Advent are found in the stories of 17–24 December.

I truly hope there is something here for you to think and pray about. I'd love to think you would share some of the thoughts with family members and friends so that a conversation above and beyond the shopping days 'til Christmas might take place. This is truly a special time and, together with like-minded people, I believe much can be done to reclaim Advent as a time of spiritual preparation.

May God bless your Advent journey. I am grateful to those who have shared my own journey, some of their stories are found in the pages that follow, interwoven with the sacred story that, in truth, is the foundation of ours.

Vincent Sherlock

First Sunday of Advent

How Many Sleeps Till Christmas?

Isn't it so hard to wait? We are forever impatient with waiting, be it at a traffic light, in a queue for a bus or at a supermarket checkout. How much more difficult it is to wait when we are looking forward to something! How many times have we heard from the lips of a child that they are six-and-a-half or, better again, 'nearly seven'? It doesn't end with childhood, we continually look forward – the expectant mother speaks of her due date, the county team of the third Sunday in September and so it goes. Yes – it's hard to wait.

Little children sometimes talk of waiting in terms of sleeps – as we begin Advent, we could wonder how many sleeps there are till Christmas. It's as if it's easier to wait and cope with waiting when we are asleep! Yet the gospel clearly calls us to be awake; more than that, to 'stay awake' so maybe that's the way to meet Advent. Yes, allow for sleep, for rest and reflection but use the waking hours too, to prepare and observe, to transform and be transformed.

Who can we notice today? What can we notice about ourselves and our attitudes? What can we see in others that might need – demand – a bit of our time? It could be a tear in someone's eye or a quietness that seems to want to find a voice, seeking an open ear. Maybe it's a church that we rush past whilst half blessing ourselves that's saying, 'Look, my door is open and you have a bit of time, come in and stay a while.'

Certainly it's not about how many shopping days are left

until Christmas or 'When a Child is Born' playing through the shopping centre's sound system in October. Neither is it about endless shopping, wondering about the size of the turkey or booking a holiday. There is absolutely nothing wrong with any of these but the timing isn't right. We are beginning a journey today that has to be taken, one spiritual step after another, day by day, sleep by sleep, waking after waking, until the destination is reached.

Take your time with it. Give your time to it. Prepare – journey with Advent!

A Moment to Pray

Lord,
On this first day of Advent, give me the grace to slow down. Let me travel with the Wise Kings, following the rising star and seeking advice as I travel. Let me select gifts to bring that may be worthy of your saving birth and help me to encounter people along the Advent way, truly encounter them in a way that is meaningful and rooted in the Christian call.

As the journey begins Lord, I place its destination in your hands and truly pray with my entire being, that I may fall to my knees, give thanks and praise your name.
Amen.

Monday, First Week of Advent

Rooms Tidied and Guests Welcomed

The centurion couldn't have known the full and lasting impact of his words the day he asked Jesus to heal his stricken servant. 'Sir,' he said, 'I am not worthy to have you under my roof'. He meant what he said and it's in the sincerity of his speaking that the words found their path.

His words to this day are central to our celebration of Eucharist. Before we receive the Blessed Sacrament, their echo is heard. We take it a bit further and speak not of the roof of our home but the soul, the shelter of our very being and we add 'but only say the word and my soul shall be healed'.

The centurion's words were spoken from a place of recognition. He recognised in Christ one who had the power to bring hope to a desperate situation. He wanted the Lord's help, but did not feel worthy to have him in his home. In the back of his mind, perhaps, he knew the house was not all it should or could be. He wanted it to be different; he wanted it to be better for his guest, so that the welcome would be sincere and the hospitality certain.

For us, in this Advent season, we are being called to realise that the tidy soul, like the tidy house, has to be worked at. It doesn't just happen. If we truly want the Lord to come and stay a while, we have to prepare the way. It's about putting the house in order – the soul in order. Somewhere and somehow we need to hear the centurion's words again and realise his words are ours too, 'Lord, I am not worthy to have you under my roof'.

To that, we need a plan of action, a road map of sorts, to guide us on the journey.

The Sacrament of Reconciliation supplies some of that road map, its coordinates are already there for us, and the initial movement might be found in 'bless me Father, for I have sinned'.

A Moment to Pray

Lord,

It's been a while, but you know that already. It's not that I don't know, I need to speak to you in a way that I've been putting off for too long. Neither is it that I don't know how to, but for some reason I'm nervous. Where do I begin to make ready the room so that I may fully welcome you? I know you've told me there is no need to be afraid and maybe that's what I need to pray for now, just for that; take away my fears and remind me that you rejoice in the coming home as did the watching father in the powerful story of the prodigal son.

I'm moving now, the steps might be slow and uncertain but remind me that already the Father is heading for the hill, watching for me, noticing me when I may well still be a long way off.

Amen.

Tuesday, First Week of Advent

Making That Call and Friendships Renewed

The Old Testament text for today's Mass (*Isa 11:1–10*) speaks of the coming together, in friendship, of unlikely travelling mates, 'The wolf lives with the lamb, the panther lies down with the kid, calf and lion feed together with a little boy to lead them. The cow and the bear make friends.' Chances are that some of the imagery may not be ours but the reality that something positive is happening is undeniable and totally desirable.

We live in a world torn asunder by hatred, suspicion, bigotry and countless attributes that divide rather than unite, hurt rather than heal, and literally kill rather than give life. We can become numbed in the face of much of this, not least when it's on a massive scale and somewhat removed from us. Too easily we can blame or look for scapegoats. Too easily we can discriminate or brand others. Too easily we can withdraw into some sort of inner smugness that all is well in our house – my house. Is it?

Though we may not be killers or assassins, there is always the possibility that we are killing other people's spirits or darkening their world through bitterness or resentment, jealousy or hatred. We would never stand over the taking of life, and recoil from violence, but at a subtle level, we might well consign others to a living death by ignoring or neglecting them. Maybe our words drive arrows into the heart of another. What we say about people could well add to their pain and exploit their vulnerability.

In these Advent days, having looked at tidying the room, we may worthily welcome our sacred guest, as the call to be builders of peace is real, urgent and essential. Taking an honest look into our own rooms, is there anyone that would not be welcome? Is there anyone we've not spoken to or that we hold a grudge against? Is there even the slightest possibility of picking up the pieces and re-establishing contact?

If you can at all, maybe now's the time.

A Moment to Pray

Lord,

I don't fully know where it went wrong. There are times I like to think that it's not my fault and I take consolation from that. It's poor consolation though, because I miss that friendship and connection. Countless times I've picked up the phone, started a text, looked at a blank sheet of paper, slowed down the car as I came to the house, but always I pull back. I'm afraid of rejection and of facing a barrage of insults. Maybe, when I'm not sure, there's some hope there, but the chances are that I need to go to that place of hurt, extend the hand of friendship to one who has stopped speaking to me and hope that Isaiah's words might come to pass again in our day. With the cow and the bear I long for friendship, pray for it, need it, but it's not easy.

Can you guide my words Lord? Will you steer my steps and, from somewhere within, remind me of that gift numbered among The Spirit's seven: courage.

Amen.

Wednesday, First Week of Advent

There's Always One

A crowd fed – that's the bottom line in today's gospel passage (*Mt 15:29–37*). 5,000 or more, we're told, fed with five loaves and two fish. Some refer to it as 'The Feeding Of The Multitude' but at day's end it was about the feeding of each person there. Feeding, and feeling of being full, can only truly be experienced on an individual level. Yes, he or she may well be part of the 'multitude', but it remains a personal experience. We could well be in the midst of a large crowd and fail to be touched by a graced moment like that. The mind, the heart, the mouth – the self must be open.

Matthew's account doesn't narrow the crowd down to the small boy who offered the few loaves and fish. There's something lovely in that small boy's offering. He gave what he had to give. You could imagine him feeling so joyful as his gift is brought to Jesus. How proud he must have felt when Jesus was told, 'There's a small boy here with five loaves and two fish'. You can almost imagine him looking at the people around and saying, 'That's me, I'm the small boy! Jesus has my food in his hand!' It's slightly crushing then to hear the disciple add the cautionary words, 'But what's that between so many?' The disciple, of course, was right and the chances are the small boy realised the truth of that statement when he heard it. From joy to embarrassment, pride to failure, in the blink of an eye, his head held high becoming a face lowered and blushing. No need to blush. It's the offering that makes the difference. Jesus and his blessing hands will do the rest.

What gifts have you to bring from the crowd today? Have you been holding back because you felt your offering might not be sufficient? Is there a fear in you about what others might say? All these questions have their place on this Advent day. They are as real as this Wednesday is. Their reality nonetheless should not hold us back. What can you bring from the crowd, from yourself, that can be offered to Jesus with full heart and unguarded generosity? What's your gift? Don't, not for one second, give way to any possible thoughts around you not having a gift. Look at what five loaves and two fish did for 5,000 and more – you have what it takes. Let your voice find its volume in the crowd, speak today, speak for all standing around you and say, 'I have something to give'.

As the Wise Kings continue their Advent journey with gifts of gold, frankincense and myrrh, there's a small boy taking the same road. He's wondering what gift he can bring – fit to give a king – and then he offers what he has, 'Shall I play for you on my drum?' We know the rest.

A Moment to Pray

Lord,

She may or may not have been in the crowd that day. It's likely she wasn't, for her days were filled with visits to doctors in the hope of gaining ease from a crippling pain that was only getting worse. It's likely she didn't get to taste the blessed bread and fish, or see the collecting of the scraps. The boy was there though, the boy – the child – in all of us that isn't overly conscious of what others might think. The child, free enough in spirit to do the silly thing and offer, like the widow in the temple, from the little that he had. Five loaves and two fish were more than enough because they were the fruit of a personal connection between you and one in the multitude. She was there another day though, for sure, having heard of this day and others like it, she wanted to meet you and make it personal, to touch you and be blessed. It happened. Healed and blessed, she knew that even in the crowd she had found you. 'Who touched me?', you asked. She knew, as you did, the answer.

Let me know my place among the crowd and never fear that you cannot find me there. Ask me again, 'What did you bring with you? What gift have you got for the crowd? For me?'

Amen.

Thursday, First Week of Advent

Ready for Holiness?

Psalm 117 includes these lines, 'Open the gates of holiness: I will enter and give thanks.' Who among us would not want to be known as holy? One dictionary definition says to be holy means to be 'dedicated or consecrated to God or a religious purpose'. How are we measuring up to that definition?

One word stands out in particular to me: dedicated! Chances are that we can handle dedication as we align it to our lives in other areas – dedicated to our family (nothing we'd not do for them); dedicated to our job (countless hours given); dedicated to sports team (no distance too far to travel for a game); dedicated to fashion (take a look in the wardrobe). Dedication and being dedicated are within our comfort level.

Dedicated to God? Now, that's another story! Nothing we'd not do for him, countless hours given, no distance too far to travel, look in our wardrobe (well maybe in this case look at our library, on the bookshelf) – what do we find? It's likely He'd not compare too favourably with some of the other aspects of our lives that are at the receiving end of our dedication. Maybe time is the dimension we most begrudge? Even the Mass-goers among us begin to look at the watch after forty minutes or less!

Another key word in the definition is 'consecrated', which is another story altogether. It's not a word you'd use about a pastime or hobby, a sporting team or even family. It's a God-word really and yet it has its certain place on our journey of faith. 'Open the gates of holiness: [dedication and consecration] and I will give thanks'; if we truly want them opened, we have to be prepared for what happens when we walk through the open gates. We need to be dedicated or consecrated to God.

'I'm spiritual, but not religious', is a comment in popular usage now. It seems to be something to do with believing in a spiritual presence out there and within but not attaching to this belief the need to worship in community or be dedicated or consecrated to a 'religious purpose'. Going back to the boy in the crowd, to the woman in the crowd who gave and received from their places *in* the crowd, there is a call to be involved with a community of worship – it's part of parish life.

Is that something to think about this Advent day?

A Moment to Pray

Lord,
I don't always find it easy to make time for Mass or church.
Well, at least that is what I tell myself. I know, as you know,
that I could do better. I try from time to time, maybe even
weekly on occasions, but I don't always feel that connection.
I look around me and see people who distract me. Sometimes
my thoughts are not very wholesome, never mind holy, and
I don't always get what the priest is saying in the homily.
I've done my share of criticising too.: 'The church is cold';
'The priest talks too long'; 'The choir was awful', 'Another
collection!' Yet, I want to be holy – to be wholly involved
– and I know that takes time and sacrifice. Will you help

me Lord, to make time for you? Will you remind me of your sacrifice as I make mine?

This week Lord, as we look to your birth, teach me to wait a little for you and not need to be in such a rush that I could miss you in the crowd.

Amen.

Friday, First Week of Advent

A Pause for Thought

A is for Advent and A is for attentiveness. Let's spend a bit of time with that word today. Let's be attentive to attentiveness.

Going back to the story of the Annunciation (*Lk 1:26–38*) did you ever wonder about the level of detail given? We could have been told that an angel went to a house of a young girl who happened to be engaged and told her that she would become the mother of our saviour. The angel could have included the details around the pregnancy, in advanced age, of a cousin of this young woman. Had all that been said, we'd know the details but not the people involved. We are given the angel's name (Gabriel), the name of the town (Nazareth), the name of the girl (Mary) and of the man to whom she was engaged (Joseph). We are told the name of the elderly, and now pregnant, cousin (Elizabeth). This is all so deliberate and so necessary. It reminds us that our relationship with God is personal and that names and details are important.

There's a lovely moment in that gospel passage. It's just before Mary is given the news of her special calling and her role in the life of the world. Having been told not to be afraid, the next word is 'listen' and it's followed by an exclamation mark. Imagine a pause there – a lengthy pause between 'listen!' and, 'You are to conceive and bear a son'.

That pause is, in many ways, our Advent. It's that time where nothing is said, but the preparation is done for what is to follow. That pause is the call to silent prayer and re-flection. That pause is as necessary as any spoken word and stands on an equal footing with all that is said.

The exclamation mark – the pause – the need to be ready for what is to follow, all of these combined is what we need to give 'attentiveness' to this day.

A Moment to Pray

Lord,

Listen! Teach me to listen, really listen, to and for your word. Help me to listen at home as I sit with family or friends – maybe even alone. May I hear your word for me, spoken in many different ways and from different platforms. It could be in the cry of a child, the held hand of a loved one or an old photograph or memorial card. Maybe it will be in church, in the response to the psalm or a word from the readings. Chances are, I need to listen more, pause more, reflect more and allow for silence. Give me the tenderness of Mary, standing on her kitchen floor, open to God's word though she could scarcely have imagined it.

Having listened Lord, teach me to respond rather than react and give me the courage to do your will.

Amen.

Saturday, First Week of Advent

Seeing the Who

Jesus' sorrow around those he perceived to be 'sheep without shepherds' is key to our Advent thoughts this day. Seeing people 'harassed and dejected' his heart, as they say, goes out to them (*Mt 9:35; 10:1; 5:6–8*). He believes they need a presence, a spiritual presence, in their lives. His attention turns to the twelve and he sends them out to be among the people, to care for them; tending to the sick, seeking out those who are lost, feeding those who are hungry and so on. In short, he sends them to minister to his people.

Facing into this Advent weekend, thinking of the priest in the parish who may well, at this moment, be searching for a few words to share with his people, maybe it's a day to pray for priests and religious. At times, many among them may well feel numbered among the harassed and dejected, with ever increasing demands and ever decreasing numbers.

When you look at the priest in your parish, think about *who* you see rather than *what* you see. The *who* is the man that at some stage in his life felt that God wanted him to become a priest. The *who* is one that knows uncertainty, doubt and disappointment, but one who still finds faith rewarding and ministry his chosen way of life. The *who* is one that appreciates a kind word and absolutely needs the support of your prayers. If we see the priest as *what*, he becomes a function, a dispenser of services and something just to be contacted when a service is required. When Jesus sent out the twelve, he knew that the people needed them just as much as they needed the people. That truth remains unchanged.

Think now of the priest you know, the religious you know, and remember their interactions with you in life. Moments of sadness and grief, moments of uncertainty or fear, sickness or tension – moments too of celebration and joy, where was he or she? Chances are, very close to you and yours. Maybe when you hear criticism of priests or religious, when sincere, accept and understand it and empathise, but maybe when you feel it is not justified you could say, 'That hasn't been my experience' – in this, at least, you are acknowledging the path chosen in response to God's call because Jesus noticed people and felt they needed ministers in their midst.

Maybe have a word after Mass; a smile, handshake and, 'Thanks for that, we're glad you are here among us. By the way, I said a prayer for you this weekend.'

A Moment to Pray

Lord,

Remind me as I prepare for weekend Mass that the priest in our parish is preparing to meet me and carry your word to me. May I hear that word from his lips, see it in his face and may he know it in his heart. He may well feel at a loss to know how to communicate your loving message and saving word, but remind me that he's there and will, with your help, invite us in blessing and greeting, through the word proclaimed and in the breaking of bread to come to know and love you in our lives.

May I remain grateful for the ministries of priests and religious. Help me to offer support through my own prayers, and in practical ways, so that all who serve you and your Church will know, now and always, the value of their calling and the difference they have made.

Amen.

Second Sunday of Advent

Man of the Match

Bartimaeus, named in one of the accounts of his healing (*Mk 10:46–52*) was blind. In Luke's account (*18:35ff*) the man is not named but his condition is recognised and he is called a 'blind beggar'. At the end of both accounts the man can see. It's a powerful story of healing and transformation and maybe it has a place in today's reflection as we light the second candle on our Advent wreath, lessening the darkness and increasing the light.

The blind man sat by the side of the road on the outskirts of Jericho. Chances are he had claimed his spot and was known to be there. One day was more or less the same as another, depending on the occasional bit of charity and maybe even less frequent kind word. Keen of hearing, he noticed a larger crowd than usual and asked what was happening. Someone said, 'Jesus of Nazareth is passing by', and the shouting began; 'Jesus, son of David, have pity on me'. People were not impressed and told him to stay quiet, but this made him shout even louder. Persistence! Jesus has a thing about persistence – he sees it as a quality. He stopped and told the crowd, 'Bring that man to me'.

We will look tomorrow at what happened next but, for today, let's look at what has happened already. A blind man has been invited into the presence of Jesus. How did this happen? Through persistence? Yes, the man called repeatedly until he was heard. The question however is, how did he know the time was right to call? The answer is found in the person, unnamed in the crowd, who said to him, 'Jesus of Nazareth is passing by'. That person, man or woman, gave Bartimaeus the chance to ask for help. Had he or she not spoken, there was no way Bartimaeus could have known that Jesus was within earshot. That person deserves great credit, and the gratitude not just of Bartimaeus, but of all who have since heard those same words, 'Jesus of Nazareth is passing by'.

Today, put names on those people in your life. These are the people who shared with you the story of Jesus and gave you the chance to come to call upon and know him in your life. Parents? Teachers? Priests/Religious? Friends? Who are they? Remember them and pray for them today.

They shaped you and, like the Advent wreath, increased the light for you.

A Moment to Pray

Lord,

I'm sitting on the roadside with Bartimaeus. All too often, the world seems to pass me by and, in my darkness, I long to catch a word on the air, a whisper even, which might reassure and encourage me. Sometimes the only voices I hear are those Bartimaeus heard too, voices telling me to be quiet and not to make a fuss. Often they came close, too close, to succeeding and I gave up for a while wondering what the point is, but somehow the whisper breaks through the hostile crowd. Like the cream rising to the surface, settling and spreading itself over the heated contents of my cup, the word gets through. It's a memory sometimes; the way my father or mother said their prayers, the first time I said 'Amen' to Eucharist and moments like that.

I'm thankful Lord for the voice that finds its way through all the noise and points me, even in my blindness, in your direction.

Amen.

Monday, Second Week of Advent

Sight Restored

He's calling you! You'd wonder was it some of the same crowd who told him to be quiet that now were involved in calling him to meet Jesus? Maybe more than one person had sight restored that day. In any case, the calling has been done and the blind man found his feet.

Standing in front of Jesus! Let's do that now – stand in front of him. Maybe even with eyes closed, but knowing where we are.

'What do you want me to do for you?' That's what he heard. Bartimaeus, who moments earlier lived for occasional acts of kindness, hears the Messiah – the man shaped of the child for whom we wait – ask before he can ask. 'What do you want me to do for you?'

What would you ask for? We may well dream of lottery wins, but given the chance to ask Jesus for what you most need, what would that be? Deepened Faith? Health for your family? Peace? Strength? Gratitude? What words would you find? What do you most need?

The gospel man knew. He needed no prompting or time to think about it. 'Lord,' he said, 'let me see …', and then the key word, 'again'. 'Let me see again'. What a prayer! The word 'again' is crucial. It says that he had seen before and somehow along the way, had lost his sight.

Can't that be our story too? Things that were once clear to us become blurred. People, once important and close to us become distanced and confusion rules the day. Oh, to see again! Perhaps that's our prayer this Advent day – a prayer to see again.

He touched his eyes then and sight returned; 'Receive what you seek'.

A Moment to Pray

Lord,

I'm standing with him now. Standing in the shadow of the darkness in which he has lived and from which he has been called. I hear you ask, 'What do you want me to do for you?' I bite my tongue because I know it's his turn and a moment he deserves. I begin to wonder what I could ask for. Thoughts flood my mind. I see a bigger house, the mortgage cleared and more security, friendships and love blessed, good health – it's only seconds but a lot pass through my mind and I begin to realise the selfishness of my thoughts. I try to focus, to get it right – were this to be my only chance, I wanted to get it right – and then I heard him. He literally took the words, not from my mouth, but from my soul:

'Lord, let me see again.'

Amen.

Tuesday, Second Week of Advent

A Voice Cries

Remember the 'man of the match' in Bartimaeus' story? Through hostility and noise his voice found its way to an ear longing to hear and to eyes desperately seeking fresh vision. Isaiah is that man today. The first reading from Scripture is a powerful call to all of us to be proclaimers of the word and mercy of God. (*Is 40:1–11*)

'Console my people, console them', and, 'Prepare in the wilderness a way for the Lord'. Later, 'Let every valley be filled in, every mountain and hill laid low […] for the glory of the Lord has been revealed.' We never heard Isaiah speak these words but, in 1963, Martin Luther King brought these words alive again during the civil rights marches in the United States in what has become known as his 'I have a dream' speech. He said, 'I have a dream that one day every valley shall be exalted, every hill and mountain shall be made low, the rough places will be made plain, and the crooked places will be made straight, and the glory of the Lord shall be revealed, and all flesh shall see it together.'

There is something being said to us today, as we prepare for the Saviour's birth, about the need to make Scripture our own. It's not as much about chapter and verse, as it is about allowing God's word to rest deeply within that. Having found its place in our core, it may speak to us and for us in the day to day living of our lives. Valleys are still in need of filling in, mountain tops of levelling and it's only with something that we can term 'faith' that we can truly take our turn and make something of a difference in our world, local and global. The word has to be real for us.

This word, alive and active, gives us the ability to console His people and allow ourselves to be consoled. This word, alive and active, helps us find our way in the wilderness.

Think today about a Scripture passage or phrase that has helped you on your journey. Read it again, speak it again – hear it again. Having done all that, share it. God's word is to be shared.

A Moment to Pray

Lord,

Open my ears to hear your word, I mean really hear it so that it takes me to that place you need me to go. Open my ears to a word concerning peace and purpose; concerning loss and finding; concerning gathering and letting go – 'a time for every purpose under Heaven'. I want to know more about your word so that I can draw from it and be strengthened by it.

Having heard your word, Lord, give me the courage to proclaim it and the joy of hearing it proclaimed. Be with all those who proclaim and teach your word so that it may be heard, treasured and forever believed.

Amen.

Wednesday, Second Week of Advent

In Tune

They're everywhere now, the Christmas carols! Shops, television and radio, even carol services in our churches, collectors on street corners with Santa hats singing 'Silent Night'. We're half way through the second week of Advent. Let Advent be Advent – easier said than done!

Where are Joseph and Mary now? The Wise Kings and the shepherds are still on the outskirts of Bethlehem. Herod is waiting, not for the birth but the return of the Kings so that he can rid himself and the world of what he perceives to be an alternative king. Jesus is waiting for birth, to be held close in the arms of Mary and Joseph, but he's not here yet. Time must have its way.

So if this is a sort of Advent retreat we're on, how do we keep focus when surrounded by a premature Christmas? Were you ever in company – loud company – but in the presence of one friend that you really wanted to talk to? There's so much going on and it's virtually impossible to hear. Yet the need to talk is real. Maybe it's been a while since you had the chance. To walk outside would be an option but it might be rude or impractical so you're in the company, the buzz and the noise and somehow you manage to have that conversation. It might be a strain but it's worth it.

Could it be something like that now? It might be rude or impractical to ignore the forced Christmas around us, but there's still value in wanting to have a conversation with Advent. Talk to it today – to Advent, to the ability to wait when waiting is the only option. No need to shout above the noise – maybe it's part of the story too. Neil Diamond has described noise as 'beautiful' and spoke of it 'begging for me just to give it a tune'.

Maybe we can hum a tune around Advent!

A Moment to Pray

Lord,

'And it's beggin' for me Just to give it a tune' – I never really thought of it like that before! The noise is everywhere and so often I try to run from it. I make my share of it too, I know that, but at times the noise gets in on me and I want quiet. These Advent days are trying to give me some quiet, some time for myself, and are asking me not to get too caught up in the rush. The rush; where has that come from? You're not asking me to rush! Some of the noise is though, so maybe I'll slow it down – help me to find a suitable 'slow air' to accompany it.

We can do this Lord!

Amen.

Thursday, Second Week of Advent

The Kingdom Alive

'The child in my womb leapt for joy', is before us today (*Mt 11:1–15*). John The Baptist, the one who recognised the Christ when they were both still in the womb; as he recognised Christ, so now Christ recognises him and says, 'Of all the children born of women, a greater than John the Baptist has never been seen' – high praise for sure, but then he adds, 'Yet, the least in the Kingdom of Heaven is greater than he is.' It seems almost contradictory, yet the point being made is that John fulfilled God's plan and sought to follow it to the very point of giving his life and, in Jesus' view, anyone who seeks to please God and merit a place in the kingdom is greater than John. Maybe we shouldn't focus too much on the greater part, rather the call to desire and seek a place in the Kingdom of God.

What is the Kingdom of God? This is not an easy question to answer. Once it was described in terms of somebody witnessing a downpour in a busy city on a crowded shopping day. The rain caught people off guard, and as people huddled together for shelter, it was noticed that young lads walked towards a boy in a wheelchair and helped his mother get him in out of the rain. Another man held his jacket over his wife's head as the icy rain soaked through his shirt and inched its way down his back. A girl stood from her sheltered and cherished doorway to offer the space to an elderly woman. A young mother wrapped her coat around her little children to shield and protect them.

All so simple but, for the one observing, every act spoke of God's Kingdom fully alive; it's about putting the other first.

The Kingdom of God is not a geographical location nor is it a walled garden. It's not somewhere to be reached but a reality to be lived. It is not about a future address but living life in the now, living it fully and alive, living it freely and cheerfully, living it for others and with others so that God's glory can reveal itself again and again, even in a winter's cloud burst.

We are part of God's kingdom, we are its cobblestones and highways, its opportunities and challenges – truly its citizens. Called to serve, called to be sincere and committed, to be convinced and convincing, tasked always with making the world a better place.

As John the Baptist was essential to the preparation of the way for Christ, know this today and always, so are you. Your attitude in these Advent days, the very fact that you reading these words, speaks of your desire to prepare the way of the Lord.

A Moment to Pray

Lord,
Remind me that I need not live in the wilderness on a diet of locusts and wild honey to be your witness in this world. Remind me that I have what it takes to make the world a better place. Yes, that might take me to the wilderness, to a few days of fasting here and there, but the real living of your gospel is in the here and now of my life. Open my eyes to see the daily opportunities to make real the Kingdom of God for those with whom I share this journey. May I recognise, in stranger and

friend, the face of your presence and hear again your words that both challenge and comfort; 'Insofar as you did this for one of the least of my brothers or sisters, you did it for me'.

Your Kingdom come; your will be done.

Amen.

Friday, Second Week of Advent

A Story Told

Mary went as quickly as she could to the hill country of Judah, she entered Zechariah's house and greeted Elizabeth (*Lk 1:39–40*). This is the story told in the second joyful mystery of the rosary – the mystery of the visitation. Isn't 'mystery' a strange word to use to describe something as ordinary as a cousin visiting a cousin? You'd see it as the right thing to do rather than a mystery. Chances are, the thinking is something to do with taking us to a deeper place of reflection – a place of spiritual mystery but, for today, let's just call it a timely visit.

It's no accident of course that Mary went to be with Elizabeth, for she had been told that her elderly cousin was also with child. Mary may well have needed a bit of space herself to get some focus on the path that had been laid before her. More than that, it's fair to say that she knew Elizabeth would need support in these days and knew she had what it took to offer that support. There's a wonderful exchange between the two of them in the recognition, in each other, of the fulfillment of God's plan. 'Why should I be honoured with a visit from the mother of my Lord?' (*Lk 1:43*) They knew what was happening, even if they didn't fully grasp all the implications.

We are told Mary stayed with Elizabeth for about three months and then went back home. We are not told much about what happened in those months, or about conversations they had, but what we are told in this time is that Mary stayed with Elizabeth for as long as she was needed. The three months would have seen the birth of John the Baptist and once Mary had helped Elizabeth to that point, it was time to go home. Elizabeth too would have helped Mary during those months. That's the way it's meant to be – accompanying another in a time of uncertainty.

As we think of this 'mystery' of the rosary today, maybe it's a day to reach for the rosary beads. It's said that if we know six prayers we can say the rosary (blessing ourselves, The Creed, Our Father, Hail Mary, Glory be to the Father and Hail Holy Queen) we have all the prayers we need. Equally, if we learn the mysteries of the rosary we have the story of Christ's life, from the Annunciation to the Resurrection. There's a lot going on in this prayer. There's a lovely line in the song 'The Isle of Innisfree' (Richard Farrelly) that speaks of a man remembering his home, the ones he loved gathered around the fireside where 'on bended knee a rosary is told'. That word 'told' is amazing – not 'said' or 'prayed' or 'given out' but *told*.

Let the rosary tell its story today and in the days to come.

A Moment to Pray

Lord,

As I take the rosary beads in my hand, remind me that Mary spends time with me as she did with Elizabeth. She accompanies me in prayer now, leading me into your presence. Help me to feel in these beads your presence passing through my fingers, continuous and linked to me as the beads are to each other. Allow me to stop, reflect and find meaning in the names of the mysteries and in the repetition of the prayers. Let me take time, as Mary did, enough time for your message to be fully revealed and then, with your guidance, put me on the road for home, never forgetting where I've been.

'May the most holy names of Jesus, Mary and Joseph, be forever praised and glorified.'

Amen.

Saturday, Second Week of Advent

Two Stories

Today and tomorrow, we will change things a little. Let us imagine someone finding this time of year difficult so that we might remember and reach out. Tomorrow might bring hope. That is Advent!

I hate being like this. I never thought I'd be like this.
Christmas meant everything to me. I put all I had
    into it
because I knew the infant gave all he had to me;
especially the infants; our children, our joy and our
    hope.
I decorated with the best of them.
I shopped for joy, hoped for peace, cooked to fill.
Joy was there, peace too and empty plates were thanks
    enough.

The cards are lovely. People write
once a year and try to share
in five lines how much they care
but there's an emptiness there
that a few xx's or a promised prayer
won't make disappear.

I hate being like this. I never thought I'd be like this.
Some say they prefer Easter to Christmas.
Never fully understood that. I thought it was
to do with weather, days being better,
nights shorter. But now …
I think it's more than that.

There's so much to miss.
Family and friends gone to God.
Neighbours' visits and negihbours visited.
Churches filled with regular faces
and … my own
who tell me now they're
'spiritual, but not religious'.

I want to deck the halls, to hear the calls.
I want to sing with the mountain-top shepherds,
drum with the drummer boy,
sing 'Glory to the New Born King'.

I'm lonely though – not alone, but lonely.
I long to see again
the lost faces of Christmas innocence
that count not time in shopping days
But time with another, for another.
How do we get to that place in this endless race?
How do we find what's been left behind.

Oh, there's the phone … just a second:
'What's that Peter? You can't come home?
You've written a card?
That's fine Love.
No, no, I'm grand,
I understand …'

Easter!

Third Sunday of Advent

Respond, Don't React!

'Peter, what's wrong?' It wasn't a usual question from his work colleague, but somehow he didn't mind that.

'I was just speaking with my mother on the phone. I told her I'd not be home for Christmas.'

'Was she disappointed?'

'She didn't say as much but I know she is. She's been lonely since my father died – it's three years now. She puts on a brave face, but I know her heart is broken. I hated making that call. I know she thought I'd be home – hoped I suppose, but the boss doesn't fully "get" Christmas and sees it as another working day. Sure you know that as well as I.

'The strange thing is I love Christmas. The even stranger thing, though my mother doesn't know this, is that I love it for what it is – God's greatest gift to the world; the gift of an infant who can bring such joy if only we'd let him. I love all its memories. I can still smell the pines of the Christmas trees my father got "somewhere" – we never asked or needed to ask! God, how hard they worked to make Christmas for us! The dinners my mother cooked, the excitement of opening the "dare to hope for" gifts from Santa. I often wonder did I say thanks …

'I remember once telling my mother that I was "spiritual, but not religious". It sounded so clever at the time though, to be honest, I still don't know what it means. I'm fairly sure I read it somewhere. I seldom miss Mass, I never go to bed without even a short prayer and my grandfather's rosary beads are always in my pocket – look!

'God, I wish she knew that for sure – my mother – that she gave me, us all, a real sense of faith. Somehow it seems unfair that she mightn't know that. I'd hate to think that Christmas might now be less for her than she made it for me.'

'Maybe I'll talk again to the boss. Certainly I'm going to talk to her about this and, as for the card I'd written, that's for the bin! For once and for all, I'm going to tell her, more than that, thank her for Christmas joy and bring it to life again for her – one way or another.

'Thanks for asking me what's wrong – it's nothing – nothing that can't be put right!'

A Moment to Pray

Lord,

On this third Sunday of Advent, the candle is pink – symbolising joy – help me to think about the two stories from Saturday and Sunday and to see them as a piece – a conversation that needs to take place. Remind me of those who find this a difficult time of year, not least because of losses felt and homes emptied. Give me again eyes to see and ears to hear, that I may notice and respond in a way that pleases you and makes better these days for another.

Amidst the purples Lord, as we move towards the whitened candlelight, may the pink – the joy – have its say in the lives of all.

Amen.

Monday, Third Week of Advent

Taking Directions

We are more than half way there. May God continue to guide the journey, the Advent trail, for you and people everywhere.

Maybe we can spend a bit of time with those distant travellers, the 'wise' ones on their journey (*Mt 2:1ff*). We don't need to get too deeply involved in the history or the geography of it, apart from seeking directions, but let us acknowledge today their thirst for salvation and their search for the Saviour.

With the best will in the world, they finished up in the wrong place. Herod's palace was certainly not the place to find the Messiah. Herod's world allowed neither space nor time for such wanderings. It was headquarters, and the feeling was there was no need to look anywhere else for power. This was the place you sought an appointment, the place you came to behold royalty and the trappings of power. Here you found servants and security, dancers and musicians, fools and sages and maybe above all, ego.

Into this place they came, seeking (as are we) to find The Messiah. The question threw Herod and his court into confusion. Advisors were brought in, people who knew the text but not its purpose, people who dealt in facts, not in faith, and they arrived at a consensus around where Christ was to be found. It was, for them and Herod, a destination, a spot on a map, but for the Wise Kings it was neither – it was destiny, fulfillment of a promise, a dream come true, but all this was beyond Herod. They left the palace and the king, in his confused glory, behind and realised the truth – that same truth we are seeking – that Christ lives among people, totally accessible for those who wish to come into his presence.

At times though, in our confusion, we might well continue to seek him in the wrong place.

A Moment to Pray

Lord,

Thinking today of the Wise Kings, the three of them, I am reminded to pray for all those in authority, that they never lose sight of the limitations of their power.

I pray that although all might not fully recognise you, they will always appreciate and support the centrality of your presence in the lives of people. I ask you never to allow the trappings of power, or the holding of high office, to confuse anyone so as to forget the long and winding road that leads us back to the borrowed stable, the journey of the kings and the 'yes' found in the heart and from the lips of Mary.

Remind me too, Lord, that in my seeking of you, like the kings, I might sometimes look in the wrong places.

Amen.

Tuesday, Third Week of Advent

Angels We Have Heard

Zechariah, the husband of Elizabeth, tending to his duties in the temple, encounters the will of God.(*Lk 1:5–25*). Uncertain, but faithful, he wants to respond positively but feels he has to ask for some form of reassurance. This led to him being silenced temporarily until God's will was revealed and fulfilled. It is not always easy to recognise or respond to God's will, and angels sometimes reveal themselves some distance from the temple.

A priest friend spoke many years ago at his first Mass. He spoke of his decision to become a priest and acknowledged the role of family and parish in that decision. The priest had been a living example of God's call and though he felt he had heard the whisperings of a vocation, he had wrestled with it. Wanting to do the right thing, but having chosen another path in life, he felt fulfilled but torn. Fulfilled insofar as he enjoyed his work, his sports and all that goes with the life of a man in his early twenties, but torn too – torn by the whispering that grew louder on occasions and seemed to be telling him he was not on the road that God had mapped out for him. He tried to silence this whispering but, unlike Zechariah in the temple, the words did not dry up. He wondered, wrestled and prayed but the road ahead became no clearer to him. All the while, he held this conversation within the confines of his own prayer life, spiritual journey and never spoke of it to anybody. In truth, he was afraid to – afraid that the truth might call for a radical shift.

Into his life came angels. Not the ones that spoke with Mary or Zechariah, well at least not in that guise. He speaks of meeting two homeless men on a Dublin street. They asked for charity but his mind was elsewhere – he ignored their outstretched hands. Within seconds he felt guilty and offered to buy them some food. Together they went to a take-away and when he gave them food, one of the men took an old miraculous medal from his pocket and offered it to him. There was gentleness in the offer and gentleness too in the refusal; "No thanks, you keep that, it will help to keep you safe." Turning to walk away, the man told us at his first Mass, one of the strangers held him in a gaze and spoke words he had never heard before: "You are going to be a priest." Life would or could never be the same again.

Zechariah didn't expect to meet the angel in the temple. My friend didn't expect to encounter one on his way to a local take-away but, as they say, 'God's ways aren't ours'. Just as well perhaps.

A Moment to Pray

Lord,

Back to Bartimaeus and his roadside prayer; 'let me see again'. How is it that I don't always remember that you are to be encountered not just in cathedral or church but often on a street corner? Jesus of Nazareth passes by and, all too easily, through the blindness of my busyness or anxiety, can be missed in the crowd. He speaks to us through angels, sent in many shapes and sizes, sent in many tones of voice – from a whisper to a roar – and all of them seeking to break through the hardened exterior so that a place of welcome may be found in the soul.

Angel of God, my guardian dear,
To whom God's love commits me here;
Ever this day, be at my side
To light and guard
To rule and guide.
Amen.

Wednesday, Third Week of Advent

Kitchen Prayers

Kitchens are great places!

So much family life is lived there. There may be better furnished rooms in the house, but there's something about the kitchen that draws us in. I like to imagine the Annunciation (today's gospel passage (*Lk 1:26-38*)) taking place in the kitchen. It seems the right room to me. The room where bread is baked, where food is prepared and the body and the soul are fed. We'll imagine her there anyway.

Who do you see when you look at Mary – Our Lady? An aunt of mine was once showing a man around her home and in nearly every room she had some picture or other, depicting (as she likes to call her) 'The Blessed Mother'. The man, possibly not overly religious, was a little perturbed and felt he had to comment: 'You have a lot of pictures of Mary,' he said. Without a flinch my aunt replied, 'oh but of course, I consider her a personal friend.' No more to be said!

It's a great way to look at Mary – as a 'personal friend' – and in that light you can see why God would dispatch Gabriel to meet her in the kitchen. He knew what sort she was. There was a generosity of spirit there and a kindness that is only truly found in the best of friends. I think that's how she would want us to see her today as we journey with her to Bethlehem in the company of Joseph. She would want us to see her as someone whose door is open to us – no need for formalities or elaborate ritual. The door is open, the light is on and she awaits our approach.

Sometimes we can put distance between Mary – the 'Blessed Mother' – and ourselves by wrapping her in too much gold and ornamentation. That's not what Gabriel encountered. He met a young woman, full of life, ready for marriage – at home in herself and by herself. She knew her story of faith and that all have a part to play in the telling of that story. In the kitchen all was revealed and within its familiar surrounds and smells she found that 'yes' that was and remains so badly needed in our world.

Queens are found in palaces. Mothers, blessed and otherwise, are found at home, like good friends.

A Moment to Pray

Lord,

Thank you for the allowing the gift of Mary, your blessed mother, into our lives. When you spoke to John, standing at the foot of the cross and said 'son, behold your mother', we are told John made a place for her in his home. That place has been assured by countless generations since that day. We are blessed to have Mary in our lives and as part of our faith story. Remind us that she found the 'yes' to fulfill your word and in that reminding, give us the courage to likewise do your will.

'Let what you have said be done unto me.'

Amen.

Thursday, Third Week of Advent

You Couldn't Have Come at a Better Time

Jack was a decent man! The sort you'd enjoy visiting. He lived alone. Well, not totally alone for he had an amazing connection with horses; a man once told me that he could leave the wildest of horses in the field beside Jack's house and within days the animal would be tame. Gentleness and patience were the only tools Jack used. He was a decent man.

I began to visit him on my first Friday calls. The priest that was in the parish before me used spread his calls over two days, Thursday and Friday, but I discovered I could do them all on the Friday. Maybe I didn't give it as much time as the other man, I'm not sure. In any case I asked Jack one day if he called in to visit any of his neighbours and he told me that he didn't. I then asked if any of them called in to visit him and again he said 'no'. He seemed quite all right with this and I asked him if he went anywhere; 'No,' he replied 'I don't bother.' 'You must enjoy your own company,' I said. 'I do for sure,' he replied and I said 'Jack, you're a lucky man.' He nodded in agreement. 'Is there anything I can do for you?' I asked. It's as if he had been waiting all his life for this question. 'Could you call on a Thursday?' he said! I smiled. The man who didn't go anywhere, didn't visit or take visitors, found Friday to be a less than ideal day for me to visit! I think we both saw the humorous side of this. We both laughed. I've never forgotten the moment. He was a decent man. I kept going on Fridays and we didn't have that conversation again.

The last time I saw him was in hospital. I just called in to see how he was doing and found him nearing the end. We said a few prayers and said goodbye. When I got to my car, I thought that I really should have anointed him so I returned to his room, said the prayers and celebrated the Sacrament of the sick with him. A few hours later his nephew called 'Jack's gone,' he said. 'May he rest in peace,' I replied. I realised it was before midnight and, more importantly, that it was Thursday. 'It took me a while Jack,' I said to him in prayer 'but I did manage to get to visit you on a Thursday.'

Today's Gospel Passage (*Lk 1:39-45*) finds Mary on Elizabeth's doorstep. Irrespective of the day, she's in the right place.

Maybe there's someone that might benefit from a visit from you this Advent Thursday?

A Moment to Pray

Lord,

As we think today of Mary's visit to her cousin Elizabeth, remind me of the importance of visitation and keeping in touch with people. Allow me that freedom of time that ensures I can visit people, especially when they most need it. May my own comforts, tiredness or laziness never stand in the way of doing right by others. May I show graciousness too in welcoming those who come to visit me and assure them of a welcome that is sincere and appreciative of the time they've given and the effort they've made.

Amen.

Friday, Third Week of Advent

Dreams Remembered

Joseph!

It would seem wrong not to give a bit of time to Joseph in these Advent Days. Scripture tells us he was an 'honourable man' and that when Mary shared with him the news she had received, he decided to leave her quietly and without fuss so that no attention would be drawn upon her. The 'leaving' may well have meant staying but not in the way he had imagined – as husband and, maybe in time, father. Like Mary, his plans were changed.

One of the interesting aspects of Joseph's encounters with the Lord was many of them seem to happen in dreams. In a dream it was revealed to him that the child Mary carried was the Messiah – the Son of God – and that Joseph need have no fears or worries about their future or their marriage. Later, in another dream, he was warned to take the newborn child to safety. Again, it was a dream that reveled to him that it was safe and time to return to Nazareth. On waking, Joseph always followed the promptings of his dreams, more than that, of course, he always followed God's will.

We imagine him these days, heading in the company of Mary and a child, as yet unborn, talking and walking, wondering and praying that all would be well. He comes across very much as provider. A strong man, skilled in his trade but with a kindness of heart and an openness of spirit that allows God's word in, even in dreams. He is the sort of man you'd like to have as neighbour and friend, dependable and kind.

Maybe today is a day to give some thought to the father-figures in our lives – those who often made great sacrifices for us. We might not always have realised the depths of their inner thoughts and concerns or maybe even the pressures they were under but we knew they were there for us. They were hard working providers, caring for the family often at great personal cost to themselves.

Thinking of Joseph today, let us offer a prayer around fathers. It might be a remembrance or a word of gratitude.

A Moment to Pray

Lord,

'Being an honourable man' or woman – isn't that a lovely description of a life choice? Please help me to be honourable in my dealings with people; courteous, cheerful and giving. May I seek to put others first, whenever and wherever possible, so that they may know always the value of their worth. Give me something of Joseph's faith, that I may hear, recognise and seek to fulfill your will Lord, even if revealed to me in dreams. Grant me an open heart and mind that your word may enter in, unhindered and ever welcome. With Joseph the Worker, may I do all in my power to work for the building of your Kingdom and support all those who work to further your message, to support and provide for families and make our world a better place.

Amen.

17 December

Old Photographs

A number of years ago, at one of our diocesan gatherings, we were addressed by Padraáigín Clancy, who devotes her life to the study of Celtic spirituality. She told us she was once at a festival in Kerry and very much enjoying everything that was happening there, when she met a man who asked her '*ce leis thú?*' An Irish question which could be understood to mean 'who is with you?' She said she was on her own. The man insisted she wasn't.

Irish is an interesting language and often the literal translation of its words and phrases lose the intention behind the words. The literal translation may well have been 'who is with you?', but that was not the intended meaning of the question. The asker of the question went on to explain what he was saying and asking. The question meant 'who do you belong to?' or 'who are your people?' The man who asked the question assured her she was not alone but that she stood on the shoulders of generations past and that, everywhere she was, the people who shaped her existence were part of her presence.

Today in the genealogy of Jesus (*Mt 1:1-17*) it is as if Jesus is being asked '*ce leis thú?*' Who are your people? It's an incredible listing of names that we might, all too easily, get lost in, but and even if we do, Jesus is found in this list. It's the tracing of a path not in kilometers or miles, but in life and in flesh and blood family. There's confusion there, ups and downs as well, but also life in all its fullness. It's about our 'roots', our history and our heritage.

So today maybe the question we need to ponder is '*ce leis thú.*' Who are your people? Those old photographs in a drawer or an album find them and spend a bit of time with them. You mightn't be able to put names on many of the people in them but they've some part to play in making you the person you are today.

Acknowledge that in prayer, in memory and in faith. We are not alone.

A Moment to Pray

Lord,

At this time of year, when so much centres around the gathering of families, remind me of mine. Remind me of my parents, their parents and all who have gone before. Though I might not have known them, remind me that each and every one of them had a part to play in the shaping of my life, the handing on of faith and in making me the person I am today. Should there be need for healing or forgiveness give me the grace and the heart to offer it today. Should there be gratitude unvoiced, help me find my voice today. Remind me too, Lord, of the ones who will number me among 'their people' and may I always strive to be a good example and a source of lasting peace in their lives.

Amen.

18 December

A Room With A View

She had mentioned it to him before but for some reason brought it up again: 'You really should clean out the shed.' He agreed and said he had been putting it off for a while but with the census happening and the pressure they would be under in the days to come, he felt she was right. It was only fair to the few animals they had. They'd been lying on the same bedding for longer than he'd normally allow. He did the few bits around the Inn, made sure they had enough stock, had a bit to eat and headed for the shed.

It was a simple structure, at the back of their home and it seemed as if it had been there forever. He wondered who had built it but had never asked. As children, they played there – 'hide and seek' and other games that took them beyond the day to day life of Bethlehem. Imagination was the only toy they needed and, in the shed, it took on a life of its own. He took out the old straw and, for some reason totally foreign to his way of thinking, decided to sweep up the odd bits that he'd normally just cover over. He checked the lights and put more oil in than he might normally use. All the while, the cow and donkey watched – they too knew him to be a gentle man and he had a respect for them that they knew wasn't always found in the human kind. Kind! Yes, that's what he was a 'kind' man.

He spent longer cleaning the shed than usual. He let his mind wander and he remembered his father one time giving the use of the shed to some people that passed through the town. He wondered where those people slept that time but knew there were no complaints. 'In fairness,' he said to himself 'it's not a bad place. If I didn't have the few animals, I often thought it would make a nice room.' Then he looked at the two, as they chewed away and said 'don't worry, as long as you're here, this shed is for you – you alone.' He thought again about his father offering shelter all those years ago. Strange, he hadn't thought of that in years …

'How did you get on cleaning the shed?' she asked him that evening. 'You should see it,' he replied, 'amazing! It's fit for a king!' They laughed.

A Moment to Pray

Lord,

Is there a room somewhere in the corner of my life that I've pulled the door on and not looked into for a long time? A room where once I wasn't a stranger or afraid? A room that had its place in my life but for some reason, I just let it fall into a bit of neglect? Do I hear today a distant sound, calling to me to tidy out this room, to make it ready for it may well be needed in a way I don't fully understand?

Give me courage and determination Lord to open the door again and spend time in that room – that space – that I may tend to it, clean and purify, prepare and leave ready for your coming presence.

A room – a room called 'soul'.

Amen.

19 December

Eye on the Ball

'Vincent', he called me by name, 'look,' he said, counting his five fingers, 'I have that many more days to spend here.' It was his first day in primary school and he was about five years of age. I called in to visit and he knew me as I was a friend of the family and a priest in his parish. He was excited to be there but, even on Monday, was counting down to Friday.

We met again recently. We were both at a wedding and when I walked into the reception, he came over to me and asked if I'd be leaving early as he had 'training for the county' in the morning. I told him I would and we arranged to travel home together after the meal. I looked forward to chatting with him.

Looking forward is such a key part of our lives. As a five year old he looked forward to Friday and freedom from the classroom. I now found myself looking forward to catching up with him and recalling some stories we shared along the way. It's good to look forward and that's what we are doing again these days. We are looking forward to Christmas and its many celebrations.

He told me that he was the goalie on the county minor team and his pride in wearing the number one jersey in county colours was obvious. He spoke freely and assured me that it was the 'toughest spot on the pitch' and that, when things go wrong, you took the flack! I asked if he had ever played in any other positions and he said 'no, I love the goals.' He had found his niche. I'm sure, like the five year old on his first day in school, he counted down the minutes too, until the final whistle – hoping his team would be on the winning side.

Today, I'd like to put the image of the goalie in front of you. He's on the line, waiting for a penalty to be taken. There are two key people on the pitch – the one lining up for the penalty and the goalie anticipating its direction. One side wanting the ball buried in the back of the net, and the other wanting a dramatic save. Until the ball is kicked and the penalty is taken there is no way of knowing which way it will end.

As Christmas draws so near now, we have to visualise ourselves on that pitch – no matter how much we want to know the outcome, we have to …

wait!

A Moment to Pray

Lord,

Looking forward is a double-sided coin because sometimes I become impatient with waiting. People talk of 'wishing your life away' and I know what they mean. When I look forward too much there is a great danger of missing what needs to be seen and done today.

Grant me patience Lord that I may, at once, look forward but also live and enjoy the now. Is that what you were saying to Martha when you told her she worried and fretted over so many things when only one thing was important?

Help me Lord to wait knowing that all the wishing in the world won't take a single second from the clock of your eternal time.

Amen.

20 December

Tinsel and Tenderness

He was found dead. People spoke with genuine sorrow and more than a little regret. He kept to himself. He'd moved from England. He used sit on a park bench and some would say hello to him. His little house seemed so small on the evening news. The houses around looked bigger but the TV camera is focused on his. He's not there anymore.

Someone walking the footpath in the middle of March noticed something and wondered.

The emergency services were called and they had to break in. The Christmas tree was on in the kitchen and the Christmas decorations still up. He had been taken down but the decorations stayed in place. The camera focused on a bit of tinsel.

It's sad of course but sadly understandable too. It could happen anywhere. Some people are very private. They keep to themselves a lot. Maybe that's the way they want it. We rush too and mightn't always notice things.

What's happening on Coronation Street? Fair City? Neighbours? East Enders? Home and Away? It seems strange that we might know the ins and outs of these fictional places but know very little about our own neighbours and community.

A Mercedes hearse takes him away – I wondered was it the first time he was ever in a Mercedes? You'd hope he had a happy Christmas – he must have wanted one – he put up decorations.

God rest his soul.

There's a thought here somewhere around 'noticing' – not prying or interfering but noticing in a positive and caring way those around us.

A Moment to Pray

Lord,

As I put up Christmas decorations this year, help me to remember this man and to be thankful for those who will share my decorated home in the days to come. Direct my thoughts and actions that those who might all too easily be overlooked may know they are cared for and loved. Give me decency of spirit that I might respond to charitable appeals and help others to have something of the Christmas I hope for.

Remind me again that it is 'in giving' we truly receive.

Amen.

21 December

Shared News

The text from a friend – a classmate – said that he wasn't sending Christmas cards but wanted to wish me peace and blessings at this special time. I called him back and asked if he was getting mean in his old age. I continued to joke with him for a little while and then he said, 'you mustn't have heard that my mother died.' I hadn't. He went on to say she died at the beginning of December. He told me his mother had been diagnosed with cancer and died shortly after the diagnosis was given. Needless to say, I was sorry for him.

I told him I'd not heard and of course he knew that because, had I heard, I'd have been there for him over those December days. The reality was the news never reached my ears and I was sorry about that too.

As we enter the final days of Advent, maybe we could remember him and how easy it is not to hear news. Gossip is all around us and seems to blow easily on the wind – easily and dangerously – but often the news we need to hear passes by unheard or untold. I wondered does God feel that way sometimes, not least around Christmas and wondered how it is that this story, this very sacred story, can remain unheard and untold.

It's the choice of this season in many ways; to hear and be shaped by the news or to settle for gossip. I know which we're called to and I know how easily we can ignore or park that call. We need to be people of the good news, tuned in to what is real and important in life, otherwise we miss opportunities to be better people, to be with people when they most need us.

Share the news. Avoid the gossip ….

A Moment to Pray

Lord,

We were never closer to news: internet, smartphones, twenty-four hour news channels, local radio, and so many more outlets. Yet, we can miss what we most need to hear. Place in me a deep desire to keep in contact with people so that in their time of need, I may be there for them. Help me to avoid, at all costs, the terror that is gossip for it is amongst the most destructive of weapons and leaves scars that run deep into the soul and long into the memory. May my words, thoughts and actions be aligned with yours, that I might cause no deliberate hurt to another.

Amen.

22 December

Do This in Memory of Me

Donal Walsh has been an inspiration to countless people. A teenager, from near Tralee in Co. Kerry, he came to national prominence during a television interview on a Saturday night chat show. It was incredible television, not least because the interviewer allowed him speak and use his time to the greatest advantage, without unnecessary interruption or distraction. Donal was dying. He spoke about how much he loved life and pleaded with people, especially young people, to put aside any thoughts around not living their lives through to their natural end. There was, in his world, too much to live for – even in his illness.

The night before Donal died, he asked his local priest what the 'other side' would be like and the priest answered: 'Donal I'm not sure but I can tell you that it will be a much better place because you are there.' It was an amazing answer to a very real question. There's no doubt the truth was spoken. There's no doubt either that Donal has realised that truth in eternity, just as he grasped many other truths while journeying with family and friends through his illness.

Since his death, his family has been heavily involved in promoting Donal's message. Travelling the length and breadth of Ireland and beyond, speaking in schools and churches and anywhere they find people willing to listen and open to his message. His work and passion for life lives on in the hearts of those who knew him most and had the greatest to lose in his dying. Truly, they are witnesses to a life well and fully lived.

Donal spoke of the mountains and hills around his Kerry home and the constant need to climb. Jesus too, when he wanted to fully reveal himself to those important to him, climbed a mountain that his glory might be seen.

I live in a part of the world that is surrounded by mountains. I can't turn my head without finding a bloody hill or mountain and I suppose those were God's plans for me. To have me grow up around mountains and grow climbing a few too. And that's exactly what I've done, I may have grown up in body around them but I've fully grown and matured in mind climbing his mountains.

— Courtesy of donalwalshlivelife.org

As we prepare for the birth of Christ, we leave ourselves open to his life-altering words as well. Like Donal, the future will treat the newborn child in ways not sought after or desirable but through it all his word will prevail. Through his word, there will be others to pick up and carry on the message so that one by one, bit by bit, the world may come to know the true value of life.

A Moment to Pray

Lord,
Remind me that there are words and messages that must not be allowed fall into silence or risk being lost in distant memory. When I hear something helpful to me, that gives me strength for my journey, allow me to bring it with me and to share it with others, that they too may come to realise the wisdom of a child, the courage of one struggling and the hopes of one from whom hope appears to be taken. May the good words of others become a central part of my vocabulary so that their good words – and deeds – live forever.

Amen.

23 December

Red Cars and Christmas Stars

Fr John Casey was a priest in my home parish. He was a curate in Cloonloo (Co. Sligo) and I never met him. He died nearly a quarter of a century before I was born. I grew up feeling I knew him though, and he has been part of my life – as sure and certain as any person I number among my friends and family. He mattered to me and still does. That's why I want to bring him to the pages of these reflections. I think he has a story to tell.

My mother spoke often of Fr Casey. She concluded every prayer we said as family, or maybe just the two of us in a car, with the words 'an Our Father and three Hail Marys to ask Fr Casey to ask God to help us and keep us free from accidents and harm at home and on the road.' This was her 'optional extra' to any prayer she said. Fr Casey mattered to her and it seemed important that his memory would matter to us as well.

She told me once that on Christmas Day (1930) Fr Casey walked into her home with Christmas gifts for her two younger brothers and herself. It was the first Christmas after their father had died and he wanted to bring a little kindness to their home. She even remembered the toy he had bought for her – a small red car. This act of kindness seems to have been at the heart of my mother's absolute wish to keep Fr Casey's memory alive and fresh for all of us. It wasn't until my own mother died a few years ago that I made the connection with the full significance of this story.

She was born in 1923 so her father died when she was about seven years of age and she was the oldest. It became clear to me then, why a priest, an obviously good and holy priest, would want to do the right thing by a young family facing into Christmas Day without their father.

Fr Casey died in 1939, and my mother some seventy years later. She never allowed his story or the place he held in her memory to be lost or forgotten. There's a question here I believe, in seventy years' time for what will we be remembered?

As we face into Christmas Eve now – the shopping is done, the food has been ordered, the travel plans have been made and the decorations and tree are in place and working – concentrate now on the story 'this is how Jesus Christ came to be born' (*Mt 1:18-25*). Make it your own, take it to your heart and remember that Christ comes to you this Christmas to bring joy and peace to you and yours, to your home and parish and to our country and world. Tell this story, retell it so that generations to come may come to know it as theirs too.

A Moment to Pray

Lord,
You told us that we ought to treat others as we'd wish them to treat us. Give me the grace and the time to reflect on that over the coming days. The young girl at the checkout in the shop – rushed and stressed – did I show respect and gratitude in the simplest of all Christmas gifts, a smile and a thank you? The carol singers down the street, is it totally necessary that their noise gets in on me or could I think that they are at least

bringing a hymn to the market square? Remembering when I last felt ill at ease or nervous and grateful for a kind word, please Lord remind me to respond in the same way. A way that is gracious and giving. Above all Lord, may I sow seeds of kindness today that will produce fruits in the memories of those with whom I share my life and for whom I live, long, long into the new day of generations to come. May I truly treat others as I'd wish they'd treat me.

Amen.

Christmas Eve

The Script Goes On

Knock Knock! Who's there?

How many times we've heard that introduction! The knock is central to this day. Joseph and Mary, strangers in Bethlehem, were searching for a place to rest, a place in which to welcome the Christ child, whose presence was drawing near. Doors opened and closed, knocks were heeded and ignored but always there was 'no room at the inn'.

A few years ago, at a Christmas Eve gathering of children in the parish, I stood beside the old wooden crib in our parish church. The children had just come, in procession, from the back of the church and placed the figures in the crib. Their parents and older brothers and sisters had taken their places in the front few seats, but the children seemed reluctant to walk away from the crib. They stayed there. I decided to go through the Christmas story with them and told them about Joseph and Mary and their desperate search for a place to stay. Refusal followed after refusal and I spoke of Joseph as he walked up to one door and knocked (as I said the word I knocked loudly on the side of the crib). I said that a man put his head out the door and said – but before I got a chance to say anything, one little boy shouted over to me 'there's no room here.' Perfect timing and when I said to him 'good boy, that's exactly what the man said', he looked back at me and said, as if I should have known this already, 'I know, I had that line in the play two years ago and it was cancelled!' Everybody laughed but he was right. Two years earlier there was a particularly bad winter and the roads became impassible. The nativity play, well-rehearsed and ready for performing, had to be called off along with many other events. His line had remained unspoken. That is, until that moment!

It's an amazing truth that we all have a line in God's drama. It may well be hidden somewhere or we may even think we've forgotten it altogether but it is there. For my young friend the knock on wood brought it back to him and he delivered it with greater effect than and at a time that he could never have imagined or planned. That's the way God works.

What is your line in this drama? What might it take to bring it to your lips this day? So that its full purpose might be realised and the impact it is capable of be reached?

It is never too late to remember it, and it is never too late to use your line. Nobody else can deliver it as well as you.

A Moment to Pray

Lord,

Remind me that what I do today might seem mundane and maybe even unnecessary, but the benefits may only truly reveal themselves through the passage of time. The inn-keeper, in cleaning his shed and taking that extra bit of care, paved the way to welcome the Saviour. During these Advent weeks, Lord, I have sought to prepare the way too and to make ready the room of my soul that I might truly encounter your presence this Christmas. May I truly behold you, O blessed infant, and welcome you with open arms into my present.

I pray for all families at this time of year, that harmony may envelop their lives and homes and the shelter of your abiding presence might banish discord, enrich family life and bring our faith to a lived reality where we will be known as Christians by our love.

Amen.

Postscript

They Walk to the Back of their Home

The shed is alive …
Shepherd boys
A young drummer
A smiling mother
Others, they're told on the way.

The animals there too
Breathing warmth on one so new
The man who had knocked and asked for a bed
The one that was almost sent on his way
But then – the change of heart
The shed was offered
The right thing to do of course
Especially when they saw the young woman
A breath away from giving birth to new breath
How could you leave them in the cold?
The two of them there now
No longer two but three
On bended knee
He looked at his Infant guest
Thankful he'd done his best
And walked back to the house

She looked at him
And smiled
'Now,' she said
'aren't you glad you cleaned the shed?'
He was.
We are.

It was the only way to prepare …
To clean
Be clean

Fit for a king

Amen!